I LIKE WEIRD ANIMALS!

Flying Geckos and Other Weird Reptiles

Series Science Consultant:
Dennis L. Claussen, PhD
Professor of Zoology
Miami University
Oxford, OH

Series Literacy Consultant:
Allan A. De Fina, PhD
Dean, College of Education/Professor of Literacy Education
New Jersey City University
Past President of the New Jersey Reading Association

Carmen Bredeson

CONTENTS

WORDS TO KNOW

chameleon (kuh MEEL yuhn)—A lizard that can change its skin color.

enemy (EH nuh mee)—An animal that tries to kill or is a threat to another animal.

parachute (PA ruh shoot)—Cloth with straps that a person wears to slow down when they jump from a high place.

scales (SKAYLZ)—Thin, flat plates on the skin of many reptiles.

venom (VEH num)—A liquid from an animal that causes sickness or death.

WEIRD REPTILES

Reptiles have skin that is usually covered with **scales**.

Snakes, alligators, turtles, and lizards are reptiles.

Some reptiles look strange.

Others do strange things.

Which reptile is your favorite?

A spitting cobra can spray venom into the eyes of its enemy.

Texas Horned Lizard

Texas horned lizards have a very strange trick.

When an **enemy** gets too close, the lizard squirts blood out if its eyes!

The blood shoots through the air, right at the enemy. *Splat!*

The enemy runs away.

ALLIGATOR

Baby alligators hatch from eggs.

Their mother scoops up the babies in her big mouth!

She carries them to water.

The little alligators learn to swim.

Sometimes they sit on their mother's head.

A chameleon catches a cricket.

CHAMELEON

A chameleon's tongue is longer than its body.

The tongue folds up in the lizard's mouth.

When a bug flies by, the tongue shoots out FAST!

It grabs the bug. *Gulp*.

ALLIGATOR SNAPPING TURTLE

A snapping turtle hides in a pond.

It opens its mouth wide.

The turtle has a wiggly pink tip on its tongue.

The tip looks like a worm.

Fish swim by and try to eat the worm.

OOPS! The turtle eats the fish instead.

This boa is eating a rat for dinner.

Boa Constrictor

A boa constrictor [kun STRIK tur] wraps its body around and around an animal.

The snake squeezes the animal so it cannot breathe.

Then the boa opens its jaws WIDE.

Slowly the snake swallows the animal whole.

FLYING GECKO

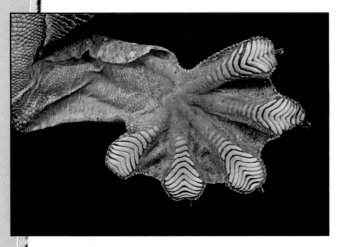

A flying gecko LEAPS from a branch.

Flaps of skin on its body spread out.

The flaps work like a **parachute**.

They help the lizard slow down.

The lizard's sticky feet grab another branch.

ruffle

FRILLED LIZARD

A frilled lizard has many folds of skin around its neck.

Here comes an enemy!

The lizard opens its mouth.

Then it fluffs up its huge neck ruffle.

This makes the little lizard look MUCH bigger.

It scares away the enemy.

HOGNOSE SNAKE

When an enemy gets near, the hognose snake plays dead.

The snake rolls over on its back.

Its tongue hangs out of its mouth.

Then the snake shoots out stinky poop to make the enemy run away. ICK!

This hognose snake is pretending to be dead.

LEARN MORE

Books

Facklam, Margery. *Lizards Weird and Wonderful*. New York: Little, Brown Young Readers, 2003.

Macauley, Kelley. *Reptiles of All Kinds*. New York: Crabtree Publishing Company, 2006.

Schulte, Mary. *Snakes and Other Reptiles*. New York: Children's Press, 2005.

LEARN MORE

Web Sites

Enchanted Learning
<http://www.enchantedlearning.com/subjects/reptiles/printouts.
  shtml>
Learn about reptiles with fun printouts and puzzles.

National Zoo
<http://nationalzoo.si.edu/animals/ReptilesAmphibians/ForKids/
  default.cfm>
Get to know reptiles through coloring, puzzles, stories, and more.

INDEX

For my weird siblings: Ralph, Jack, and Renee

Enslow Elementary, an imprint of Enslow Publishers, Inc.
Enslow Elementary® is a registered trademark of Enslow Publishers, Inc.

Copyright © 2010 by Carmen Bredeson

Library of Congress Cataloging-in-Publication Data

Bredeson, Carmen.
  Flying geckos and other weird reptiles / Carmen Bredeson.
    p. cm.—(I like weird animals!)
  Summary: "Provides young readers with facts about several strange reptiles"—Provided by publisher.
  ISBN-13: 978-0-7660-3126-5
  ISBN-10: 0-7660-3126-8
  1. Reptiles—Miscellanea—Juvenile literature. I. Title.
  QL644.2.B73 2010
  597.9—dc22
                                2008021495

Printed in the United States of America

10 9 8 7 6 5 4 3 2 1

To Our Readers: We have done our best to make sure all Internet addresses in this book were active and appropriate when we went to press. However, the author and the publisher have no control over and assume no liability for the material available on those Internet sites or on other Web sites they may link to. Any comments or suggestions can be sent by e-mail to comments@enslow.com or to the address on the back cover.

Every effort has been made to locate all copyright holders of material used in this book. If any errors or omissions have occurred, corrections will be made in future editions of this book.

Photo Credits: © C.C. Lockwood/Animals Animals, p. 9; © Ingo Arndt/Foto Natura/Minden Pictures, p. 16; © John Cancalosi/ Naturepl.com, p. 6; © Joseph T. Collins/Photo Researchers, Inc., p. 13; © Klaus Uhlenhut/Animals Animals, p. 18; © Lynn M. Stone/Naturepl.com, p. 14; © Michael Richards/John Downer/naturepl.com, p. 5; © Minden Pictures/Getty Images, p. 21; © Raymond A. Mendez/Animals Animals, p. 7; Shutterstock, p. 3; © Stephen Dalton/Photo Researchers, Inc., pp. 1, 2, 10; Tom McHugh/Photo Researchers, Inc., p. 17.

Cover Photo: © Stephen Dalton/Photo Researchers, Inc.

Note to Parents and Teachers: The *I Like Weird Animals!* series supports the National Science Education Standards for K–4 science. The Words to Know section introduces subject-specific vocabulary words, including pronunciation and definitions. Early readers may need help with these new words.

Enslow Elementary
an imprint of
E **Enslow Publishers, Inc.**
40 Industrial Road
Box 398
Berkeley Heights, NJ 07922
USA
http://www.enslow.com